# OXFORDSHIRE COUNTRY WALKS

# 1
# EVENLODE
## AND
# WYCHWOOD

## SEVEN CIRCULAR WALKS 3–8 MILES

Mary Webb, Alan Spicer
and Allister Smith

 XFORDSHIRE BOOKS

First published in 1990 by Oxfordshire Books

Copyright © 1990 Oxfordshire County Council

ISBN 1–873222–00–9

**British Library Cataloguing-in-publication Data**
CIP Catalogue Record for this book is available from the British Library

Typesetting by PM Typesetting Ltd. Exeter

Printed in Great Britain by The Bath Press, Avon

**OXFORDSHIRE BOOKS**
**Official Publisher to Oxfordshire County Council**

An imprint of Wheaton Publishers Ltd
A member of Maxwell Communication Corporation plc

Wheaton Publishers Ltd
Hennock Road, Marsh Barton, Exeter, Devon EX2 8RP
Tel: 0392 411131  Fax: 0392 425274

SALES
Direct sales enquiries to Oxfordshire Books at the address above

# PREFACE

This series of circular walks covers part of West Oxfordshire from Blenheim Park in the east to Ascott-under-Wychwood to the west. They follow the line of the Evenlode Valley and explore the area once contained in the ancient Royal Forest of Wychwood. Several trails include part of the Oxfordshire Way long distance footpath.

The length of the walks varies between three and eight miles (5 to 13 km) and short cuts are included where possible. There are a few places where the ground may be muddy but for the most part the going is good. Obviously the time taken to follow the walks will vary with the individual, but they are designed to be taken at a leisurely pace allowing plenty of time to read the descriptions and look at the wildlife and landscape. Ordnance Survey maps 1:25000 scale will add to the interest of the trails.

This guide has been produced with the aim of showing just how much of our heritage is present in the landscape. You will see features ranging from Roman roads, Domesday Book manors, medieval trading routes, eighteenth-century parkland, nineteenth-century fieldscapes and farms and twentieth-century developments. Wildlife can be found everywhere, sometimes in the least obvious places and often with a tale to tell about the past. The introduction gives a brief background to the history of the landscape and to the origins of its flora and fauna.

We hope you enjoy discovering your landscape as much as we enjoyed producing this book.

ACKNOWLEDGEMENTS

This booklet was written and researched by
Mary Webb, Alan Spicer and Allister Smith, all of the Oxford Polytechnic,
with illustrations by Louise Spicer. The authors are grateful
for help and support from the following organizations:

Oxfordshire County Museum Services; Berks, Bucks and Oxon Naturalists' Trust;
British Rail; National Westminster Bank; Council for the Protection of Rural England;
Oxford Fieldpaths Society.

The project was sponsored by Oxfordshire County Council
and West Oxfordshire District Council.

# CONTENTS

## INTRODUCTION

## SEVEN CIRCULAR WALKS

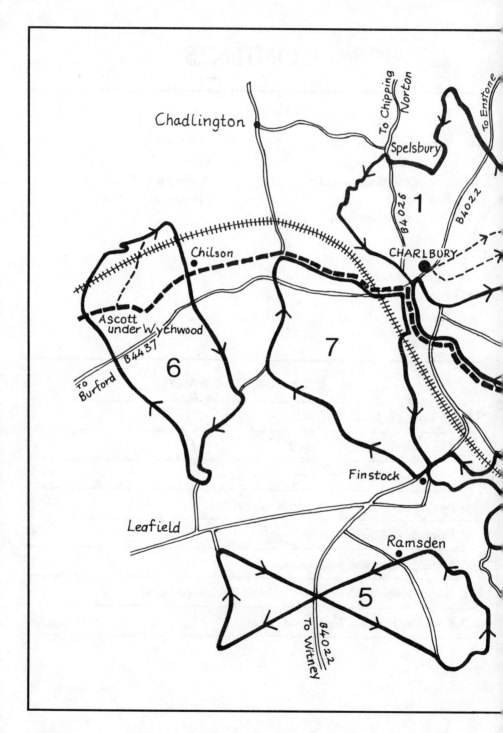

Chadlington

To Chipping Norton

To Enstone

Spelsbury

B4026

1

B4022

CHARLBURY

Chilson

Ascott
under Wychwood

B4437

To Burford

6

7

Finstock

Leafield

Ramsden

5

B4022
To Witney

**Locations of the seven walks, arrows show direction of the routes.**

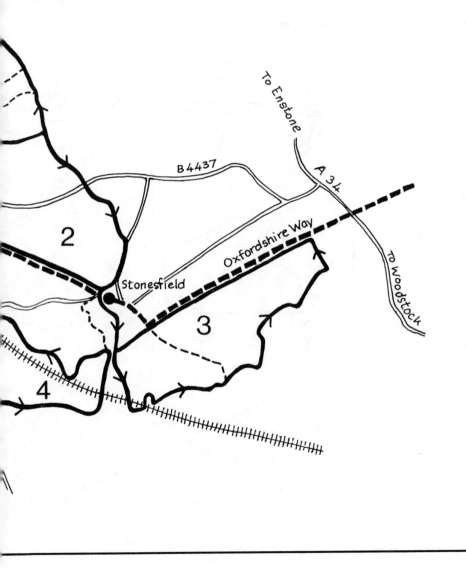

| | |
|---|---|
| ——— | Road |
| ▬ ▬ ▬ ▬ | Circular Walk |
| ▰▰▰▰ | Walk on road |
| ——— | Track |
| - - - - - - | Footpath |
| ∿∿∿ | Stream |
| ⬤ | Pond or lake |
| ■ | Building |
| ☿ | Deciduous trees |
| ⋀ | Conifers |
| ⸍ⁱ⸍ | Grassland |
| + | Church |
| PH | Public House |
| NT | National Trust |
| Spr | Spring |

Key to individual route maps

# INTRODUCTION

## History of the Wychwood Region

Man's impact on the Wychwood area stretches back into prehistory. The presence of Neolithic long barrows and later Bronze Age round barrows indicate that there were settlements here from at least 3000 B.C. The Iron Age (500 B.C. to A.D. 40) saw an increase in social organization with, towards the end of the period, the construction of earthworks such as Knollbury Camp and Grim's Ditch, which is a series of linear earthworks enclosing twenty-two square miles. No evidence of any large Iron Age settlement has been found within the bounds of the Ditch, but there is marked concentration of Romano–British villas here and it is thought that these developed from earlier Iron Age communities. The name 'Grim' occurs in many ancient places in England and is thought to be derived from the Old English word 'grim' or 'grima' meaning evil spirits, a later way of explaining the seemingly supernatural constructions. Another derivation could come from the Latin 'grumos', a heap of earth, a Roman description of the earthworks they found. Grim's Ditch can be seen on Walks 1 and 3 in this book.

There was a strong Roman presence in the Wychwood region, which was well placed on the road network with Akeman Street, based on a pre-Roman track linking Verulamium (St Albans) and Corinium (Cirencester), crossing it. The light soil was suitable for cultivation and there was a plentiful supply of timber for fuel and building. Roman buildings were first of simple rectangular timber construction, which gradually developed until by the fourth century the villas at North Leigh and Stonesfield were highly elaborate with mosaic floors, bath suites and central heating. Other sites at Ditchley and Shakenoak declined earlier but at their height would have been the centre of large estates. As well as the villas, there was a village settlement at Wilcote along Akeman Street. All these places will be seen on the trails.

After the decline of Roman control in the early fifth century, much of the previously open land reverted to woodland, so that the later Saxon settlements here were restricted to places on the woodland edge or in large cleared sites.

By the tenth century the Wychwood area had royal associations and in the Domesday Book of 1086 it was recorded as Royal Forest. The medieval term 'forest' is really a legal one and does not mean that the whole area was wooded, although there would have been some woodland as well as heath, grassland, fields and some villages, including Stonesfield and Combe. There were strict rules governing the use of the forest. The King had hunting rights over the whole area designated as Royal Forest, even though much of the land was held by various Lords of the Manor. Only the woodland at Woodstock (later Blenheim), Cornbury and a large area near Kingstanding Farm belonged directly to the King. The King could grant rights to hunt deer and wild boar to others e.g. the Bishop of Winchester. The Lords of the Manor had rights to timber and underwood while the right to graze animals (right of common) was given to the tenants and inhabitants of the surrounding villages. The size of the Forest fluctuated over time, being greatest during the reign of Henry II (1154 to 1189) when it covered most of West Oxfordshire. By 1300 it was divided into three separate portions, centred on the parks of Woodstock, Cornbury and a part which included the Bishop of Winchester's Witney estate.

Over time further clearing of the woodland (assarting) took place and often this is recalled in field names such as Gerner's Sart in Stonesfield and The Sarts in Finstock. In 1704 Woodstock Park was given by the Crown to the Duke of Marlborough and Cornbury Park was already in private hands. This left a residue of about ten square miles of Wychwood which remained Royal Forest until 1857 when a Parliamentary Act of Disafforestation took the area out of Forest Law. Within two years there was farmland on 2000 acres of previous woodland with new farmhouses, roads and boundaries, all of which can be seen north of Leafield on Walk 6. The remaining woodland was enclosed in 1864 and still exists: all that is left of the ancient Forest of Wychwood.

## The Past in the Landscape
### WOODLAND

Until quite recent times, woodland was utilized as an asset and managed accordingly to produce a steady supply of timber for building and smaller underwood for fuel, repairs and fencing. This was achieved by having a mixture of tall standard trees which were left to grow to the appropriate size for timber, and smaller, bushy trees or shrubs, which were cut to ground level (coppiced) over a cycle of years for smallwood. Pollarded trees were cut above animal grazing height and produced small poles in a similar way to coppicing. Both coppicing and pollarding extend the useful life of trees.

Wychwood was divided into compartments which were coppiced over an eighteen-year cycle and then fenced to keep out grazing animals, particularly deer and domestic sheep, goats, pigs and cattle, so as to allow new shoots to grow and provide the next supply of underwood. The most common coppice tree was hazel which was used for wattle fencing as it is so pliable, while oak and ash were common standard trees in this area. This practice of woodland management died out before the last war but is being revived in some places, especially as a means of wildlife conservation. It produces a variety of habitats during the cycle of cutting and regrowth, thus allowing flowering plants to flourish during the open phase, which then become suppressed when the tree cover is dense. Various birds and insects favour different aspects of the cycle as well, some liking scrubby conditions, others preferring a more open habitat.

### FIELDS AND HEDGES

In the fields some signs of the past can still be seen. In places where there has been long undisturbed pasture there may be remnants of ridge-and-furrow cultivation dating back to the large open-field system of the Middle Ages. The ridges were made by the ploughing methods used and acted as a simple form of drainage system. If the land was later turned to permanent pasture, then the ridges remained in the grassland. Some examples can be seen on Walk 1. Sometimes the origin of the fields can be guessed by looking at their shape and the hedge that surrounds them. Irregularly shaped, often small fields, are likely to be assarts, cleared directly from the woodland with hedges formed from strips of uncleared woodland which contain remnant flora such as wood anemone and yellow archangel. In contrast to these rich hedges, the planted hedges of the eighteenth and nineteenth centuries tend to have only one or two species, usually hawthorn or blackthorn, and have no woodland plants. These hedges were planted as a result of the Enclosure Acts, when the large open fields, still with individual strips, were divided into rectangular plots to improve crop yields and to consolidate land holdings. Earlier than this, some land owners enclosed their holdings on the open field often using a mixture of trees or shrubs taken from nearby woodland. Hedges planted originally with a single species can be dated approximately by saying that in a thirty yard stretch each species of tree or woody shrub is equivalent to one hundred years in age. However, many factors can influence the number of species so for an accurate date this biological information should be confirmed by documentary evidence.

## DESERTED MEDIEVAL VILLAGES
In the vicinity of these walks there are several sites of villages which were deserted in the later Middle Ages; Cote and Tapwell with Nether and Upper Chalford not far away in the Glyme valley. These villages were deserted for several reasons. In the twelfth and thirteenth centuries there had been a period of rapid agricultural expansion, followed by a decline, so that by the time of the Black Death in 1348/9, weak or small settlements were likely to suffer most. Due to the drop in population there was a tendency to change from arable farming to sheep pasture which was less labour intensive. All these factors contributed to the gradual decline and eventual loss of these settlements.

## ENCLOSURE
Enclosure of the large open medieval fields took place over a period of several centuries. The sixteenth- and seventeenth-century Tudor and Stuart enclosures tended to be piecemeal as a land owner consolidated his holdings. These fields tend to be long and narrow, sometimes in a reversed 'S' shape where the strips were enclosed. As agricultural improvements became more widespread with new crops and methods, so the pressure to change the open-field system became stronger especially on the part of the large landowners. Parliamentary Acts of Enclosure took place from the early 1700s for the next century or more. The land was divided into regular rectangular fields, hedged with hawthorn with some timber trees, and new farms were built away from the villages. The smallest landholders became labourers. As well as the open fields, the areas of common and waste were enclosed, the poor being given allotments to compensate for their loss of common rights of grazing and fuel collecting. New roads were laid out across the countryside and characteristically were wide enough to allow detours over impassable stretches before a hard surface was laid. Now they can be identified by their wide verges, often full of cow parsley in the late spring.

## BOUNDARIES
Parish boundaries are thought to date back to Roman or Iron Age estates and some parishes still have Anglo-Saxon charters in existence describing the bounds of the

Deer in Cornbury Park

Leafield Barrow

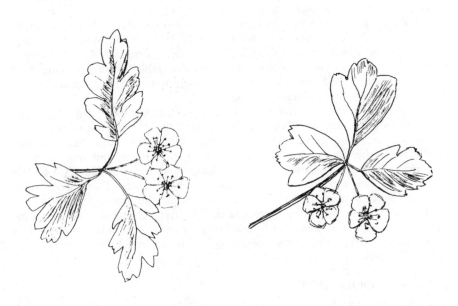

Common hawthorn and midland hawthorn

parish which can still be traced on the ground. These important adminstrative boundaries often follow natural features such as water courses or hill-top ridges, while man-made hedges, ditches and banks were likly to have been constructed after the definition of the parish and take a characteristically sinuous line over the countryside. Roads and paths often follow boundaries, either as a result of marking the bounds of a parish or else because a through route was taken between the territories of two land units.

In woodland, banks are often seen. They mark boundaries of coppice areas, as in Wychwood Forest, or can show the position of an earlier woodland edge, especially if the composition of the woodland is different on each side. The banks are usually associated with a ditch. If the ditch is on the woodland side of the bank, then this was designed to prevent the escape of deer from the wood and possibly indicates the earlier existence of a deer park.

## Natural History

GEOLOGY

The land shape is dictated by the underlying rock formation. In the Wychwood area the main type of rock is Great Oolite limestone (Cotswold Stone) laid down in the Jurassic period (195–136 million years ago). The rock was formed by the deposition of numerous spherical particles of calcium carbonate in the warm shallow sea which covered this part of Britain during this period. The limestone of the Wychwood area is harder than the chalk of south and east England, but softer than the older carboniferous limestone in north and west England, Wales, central Scotland and Ireland. Fossilized seashells may be seen in some walls in the area. Variations on this limestone include Forest Marble, a harder building stone, and Stonesfield slate, a sandy limestone which was split to make roofing tiles. Cornbrash is a rubbly type of limestone which produced the well-drained soils so suitable for corn growing. In the Evenlode valley above Fawler, Lias clay occurs, formed from deposits of dark mud in deeper water also in the Jurassic period.

Along the junction between the limestone and clay the spring line occurs. Of a series of ice ages, only the Anglian, about 400 000 years ago, reached the Wychwood area and carved a gorge in the valley near Stonesfield, although the effects of other ice ages were felt in the changes of climate and vegetation. The differences in the geology affected early settlement patterns with hamlets occurring on the spring line where there was a ready supply of water. The alluvial soils in the valley bottom were used for hay meadow while the limestone uplands were suitable for grazing pasture and woodland. The river Evenlode follows an easy course through the clay areas but below Fawler it cuts through limestone forming steeper-sided valleys, with a meandering course near Combe where it flows in a wider valley plain.

ANCIENT WOODLAND

In Southern England the natural vegetation, if left undisturbed, would be woodland, except in very exposed places such as the coast. Before the advent of man this 'wild wood' covered most of the country, but as man's influence became stronger, so the woodland started to be cleared to make way for settled agriculture. Areas of woodland remained, some untouched, most providing useful timber. These descendants from the original forest are called primary ancient woodland and are rare. Other woodland regenerated on areas previously cleared and many of these woods are extremely old. Woodland dating from before 1600 is termed secondary ancient woodland. Woods which have grown since then are secondary woodland. The ancient woods have a long history of woodland cover, even if the wood has been managed for timber production by coppicing and selective felling.

This continuity of woodland has resulted in the development of specific communities of plants which can thrive in the shady conditions, or which flourish in years of light conditions brought about by coppicing. Plants which can only spread slowly are good indicators of ancient woodland e.g. wood anemone, spurge laurel, yellow archangel, primrose and goldilocks. Certain trees and shrubs are also characteristic of ancient woodland e.g. field maple, midland hawthorn and service tree. In order to identify ancient woodland by its vegetation many such species need to be present. In places which were once thickly wooded but are now cleared, some of these indicator species persist in hedges formed from unfelled woodland strips. These help to give a clue to the age of the hedge, if the date of the woodland felling is known.

## LIMESTONE GRASSLAND

The striking characteristic of natural limestone grassland is the rich flora providing an ideal habitat for butterflies. The soil contains much calcium but few other nutrients, and is porous, tending to dry out quickly, so that tall grasses are restricted and allow other plants to flourish. These plants can tolerate the chalky conditions (calcicole plants) and often have adaptations such as hairy leaves to help reduce water loss. Many belong to the pea family (legumes), clovers, vetches, bird's foot trefoil, meddick and sainfoin, all of which can fix nitrogen from the air, so improving their nutrition.

Another factor in the formation of rich limestone grassland is the action of centuries of sheep grazing which produced a short turf, but now that sheep are no longer so dominant in the agricultural scene, and myxomatosis has reduced the rabbit population, this type of grassland is becoming threatened by scrub encroachment. The widespread use of artificial fertilizers stimulates the growth of coarse grasses and larger herbs which dominate the smaller flowery plants, so that in many places the only limestone grassland flora which remains is on steep slopes and unsprayed roadside verges.

Wychwood woodland

# ACCESS ROUTES TO THE SALTWAY
## (Walks 1 and 2)

An interesting old track leads from the centre of Charlbury to the Saltway where either the North or South trails can be taken. There are two further ways of reaching the Saltway, outlined at the end of this section. All three can be used to vary the distance of the Saltway walks.

### 1 SP358197

The walk starts at the Spendlove carpark in the centre of Charlbury. Take the road opposite the entrance, past the Playing Close which was a recreation ground as early as 1447 and continued to be used for bull baiting and fairs up to the nineteenth century.

Continue to the bottom of the hill and take the footpath on the left which follows a stream, lined with pollarded willows, to the main road. Cross the road and take the footpath opposite alongside a house called Blenheim Farmhouse and follow it through a narrow field known as Sandford Slade. The name 'slade' refers to a muddy or waterlogged area and a spring arises at the bottom of this small valley where the geology changes from limestone to clay.

### 2 SP365195

The path continues climbing up the slope through two small fields the second of which is the first community nature reserve set up by BBONT: the Berks, Bucks and Oxon Naturalists' Trust. The reserve is run by and for the local community and is an area of semi-improved limestone grassland where so far over fifty types of grassland plants have been recorded. On the left is an area of recently-planted native trees: whitebeam, cherry, oak and alder which add to the variety of species in the reserve. The scrubby woodland on the right contains flowering shrubs like hawthorn, elder and dog rose which provide nectar in the spring and summer for insects, and berries in the winter for birds. The grassland will be managed either by cutting or grazing in order to encourage the flowering plants which otherwise would be swamped by the strong-growing grasses.

### 3 SP366195

The trail continues over a stile beside spreading field maple trees, the only native British maple, more often seen as a hedge species. The path leads along the edge of a field but soon becomes enclosed on both sides. This field is to be converted into a community woodland to celebrate the completion of a century of public service by the Oxfordshire County Council in 1989.

The track is here called the Woodstock Way and before the days of the turnpike road which now links Charlbury and Woodstock, this was the lane which led to the Saltway, the ancient track between Chipping Norton and Stonesfield. The line of the hedge shows that it was once wider than now when it was more frequently used, but the encroaching scrubby woodland provides a useful habitat for wild life.

## 4 SP369197

The trail reaches a junction with another path from the left, but carries straight on. In the near distance to the left is a quarry, excavated during the last fifteen years, part of which is a geological Site of Special Scientific Interest (SSSI). It shows the succession in rock formation as layers of limestone were deposited during the Jurassic period about 164 to 170 million years ago and is the best example of Chipping Norton limestone in Oxfordshire.

Across the field to the right a large curving hedge can be seen. In the summer a better view can be had by taking a short diversion to the right at the junction. This hedge is part of the last remnant of a large wooded area, first recorded as Abbot's Wood and later known as Lee's Rest Wood, which once was part of the ancient Royal Forest of Wychwood. The shape and area of Lee's Rest Wood is shown on a map of 1797 and the present day pattern of the fields and hedges shows exactly where the wood lay, so that these hedges form the boundary of the ghost wood, felled in about 1857.

## 5 SP375198

As the path continues, evidence of the earlier proximity of woodland is shown in the adjacent field names. To the right lies Woodfield and Stump Ground, whilst, as the path bears left, the old use of the path is shown in Mile Oak Piece, showing the place where an oak marked a mile from Charlbury.

The path crosses an arable field and a few arable weeds can be seen such as shepherds purse, field pansy, poppy, plantain and pineapple weed, this last getting its name from the smell of its leaves and flowers when crushed. Many of these weeds are short-lived. The seeds lie dormant, buried after harvest, and need to be brought to the soil surface to the light before they germinate. This is why poppies are often seen on sites which have recently been disturbed after a long period.

On the horizon ahead, the woods of the Ditchley Estate can be seen. They have been in existence for centuries but many are now conifer plantations.

## 6 SP381200

Woodstock Way meets the Saltway at Dustfield Farm, which is on the site of a very early clearing in the woodland, known as Dustlefeld in 1300. Another name for the Saltway is Mereway, which demonstrates the antiquity of the track. The name comes from Old English '(ge)maere' meaning boundary and for most of its length the track forms part of the parish boundaries between Spelsbury, Charlbury, Fawler, Wootton and Stonesfield as well as between the Ditchley and Blenheim estates. The Saltway gained its name from the use of the track for transporting salt from Droitwich during the Middle Ages. It could be part of a route going as far as Princes Risborough, in Buckinghamshire, which, in the Domesday Book, was recorded as having salt-rights at Droitwich. The width of the track shows its long use as a drove way for animals, especially sheep.

Turn left to follow Walk 1, Saltway North, and right for Walk 2, Saltway South.

# ALTERNATIVE ACCESS ROUTE 1

Turn left up the hill from the Spendlove Centre, past the Recreation Ground to the road junction. Turn right here, past the Youth Hostel, once a glove factory, and then immediately left along Ditchley Road. (On the way the road bends several times, after the third bend, it follows the route of Grim's Ditch for a time.) This leads to the Saltway, joining it at the lodge gates at the entrance to the Ditchley Estate (SP380206).

# ALTERNATIVE ACCESS ROUTE 2

Again, turn left from the carpark, up the hill. At the junction keep straight on for a short distance before taking a path slightly to the right called Hundley Way.

It is thought that this track formed the boundary between the large open common fields which were cultivated during the Middle Ages until enclosure took place. It divided the land of Charlbury fairly evenly into two portions, the North Field and the South Field. A map of 1761 shows that none of the land holdings cross this track, so that it probably dates back to the time of the formation of the fields in Saxon times. The track meets the Saltway at SP377210.

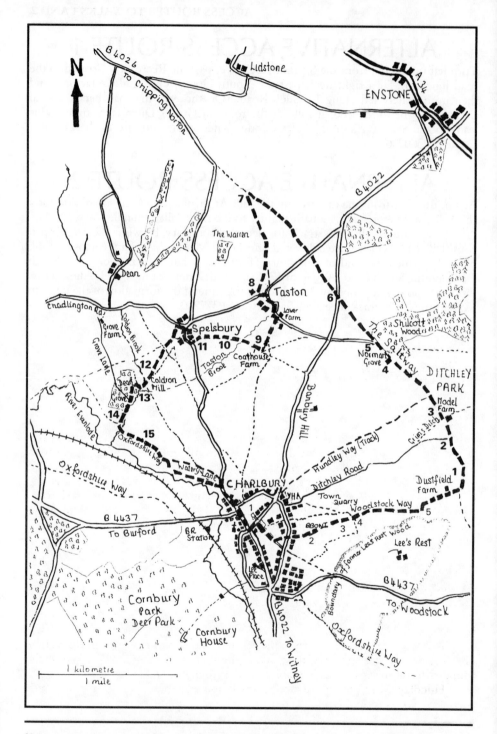

# WALK 1

# SALTWAY NORTH

*8 miles (13 km)*

Reaching the Saltway via one of the three access routes described earlier, the walk follows this ancient drove track, then descends into the Evenlode valley through Taston and Spelsbury, leading back to Charlbury through an area of ancient woodland and a series of old fields and lanes.

## 1 SP381201

Turn left at Dustfield Farm from Woodstock Way. The flora of the Saltway is obviously much richer than that of the field path you have just walked. See how many different flowers you can find, but don't pick them! A little further on there is a new plantation with a mixture of conifer and beech. Notice the different types of cones on the conifers. The male cones are in clusters and release clouds of pollen in the spring. The females take three years to mature; the youngest pinkish cones are at the ends of some branches, while the second years are bright green, becoming the familiar woody grey-brown cone ready to release seeds by the third year.

## 2 SP380206

A road from Charlbury meets the trail and enters the Ditchley Estate. (If this is your access point, turn left here.) Ditchley has a long continuous history beginning with a Roman villa, which was the centre of an estate of a thousand acres and was used into the fifth century. The name Ditchley dates from Saxon times and means 'the clearing (leah) by the ditch' referring to Grim's Ditch which will be seen shortly. The estate was bought by Sir Henry Lee and made into a park in 1605. A mansion and landscaped grounds still exist, where, during the Second World War, Churchill relaxed away from the public eye.

## 3 SP379208

At Model Farm a path leads off to the right through the farm yard. By following this short diversion, Grim's Ditch can be seen in a strip of conifers on the left. It is in the form of two earth banks with a ditch between, but in the sumer is hidden by vegetation.

Retrace your steps to return to the Saltway and continue in the same direction as before. Along this stretch of the Saltway, look out for plant species which prefer a lime-rich soil such as cowslip, scabious and St John's Wort.

Hundley Way, the third access track joins the Saltway near here. (See alternative access route 2)

## 4 SP374214

Opposite a house called Norman's Grove, over the stone wall, remains of a pond are still apparent with some old pollarded willows growing alongside. The hedges are covered with black bryony, with shiny arrow-shaped leaves. The bright yellow and red fruit is poisonous but is eaten by birds after it has been frosted during the winter.

Shilcott Wood on the right is a remnant of ancient woodland, although mostly replanted with conifers. Sweet woodruff can be seen along the woodland edge in May with tiny white flowers. The dried leaves are vanilla-scented and were used to freshen medieval dwellings. There are many large beech trees in this vicinity. Look for brown dead tips on many of the leaves which are caused by the larvae of beech miner weevils, which, as their name suggests, burrow through the leaf tissue, damaging the veins, causing the tips to die.

## 5 SP370217

Keep to the right as the track forks. The trail becomes more open as it emerges from the edge of Shilcott Wood and descends a gentle slope.

A hump, more obvious in the winter when the grass is short, is the remains of an outlier of Grim's Ditch which could be traced across the neighbouring fields from the edge of the wood until the marks were ploughed out.

The grassland in this area is full of flowering plants including hedge bedstraw, which belongs to the same family as the woodruff seen at the woodland edge earlier. Yellow rattle which is parasitic on grass can be found. Its gets its name from the large seeds which rattle inside the flattened fruits when ripe. Some scrubby plants like dog rose and hawthorn are starting to spread from the hedge so that occasional cutting would be a good thing to maintain the flowering plants and stop the take over by scrub.

This flowery area is ideal for butterflies during the summer. Look out for black and white marbled whites, meadow browns and very dark brown ringlets as well as fast-flying skippers, triangular in outline. The caterpillars of all these species live on grasses. You may also see common blue, whose larvae feed on bird's foot trefoil.

## 6 SP367221

The track crosses the Charlbury – Enstone road and continues with good views on the left-hand side across to the present-day Wychwood Forest to the south and to the Burford – Stow ridge on the skyline to the west.

After crossing the Taston – Enstone road, the ground becomes rather sticky as the soil is clay. A nearby field is called Brickground and the long disused small quarries in this vicinity, also remembered in the field name of Second Slat Pits, indicate that in the past this small area must have been quite an industrial site.

In the tall hedges, look out for buckthorn which provides food for the larvae of the bright yellow brimstone butterfly, which hibernates to emerge on warm sunny days in early spring.

The track climbs slightly and on the right is a small nineteenth-century byre. Notice the semi-circular cope or top to the wall. Shaped stones are often a feature of the soft-stoned Cotswold walls; look out for more in Spelsbury.

At this point turn left off the Saltway down a field path.

**Blenheim Farm Nature Reserve**

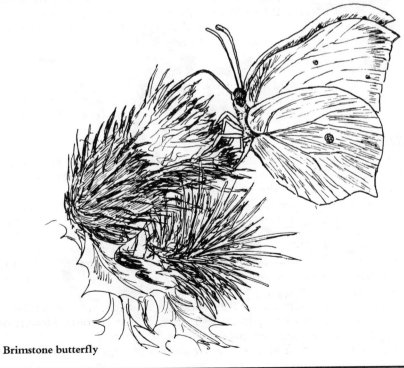

**Brimstone butterfly**

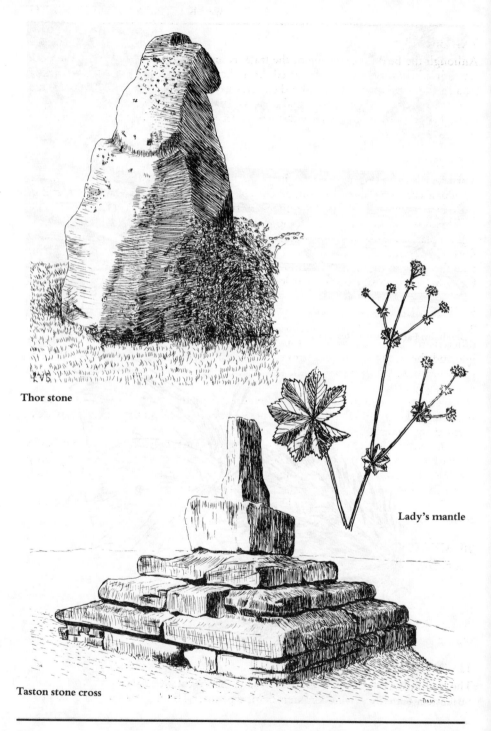

**Thor stone**

**Lady's mantle**

**Taston stone cross**

## 7 SP361229

Although the field on each side of the track is under intensive cultivation, the flora on each side of the path is quite varied throughout the summer. Look for medick, a small yellow clover which can be distinguished from other similar clovers by the serrated tips of the leaves which make an 'M' shape.

The path leads downhill with views over the valley through pasture fields to the tiny hamlet of Taston.

## 8 SP359221

Turn left at the barns and then right at the junction. Follow the road through the village. Taston gets its name from an ancient standing stone, the Thor Stone, still in place in a cottage hedge near the remains of the old village cross.

Following the road through the village, a spring can be seen on the left. This is a good place to see water-loving plants such as watercress, figwort, yellow monkey flower, liverwort and mint. After a left-hand bend in the road, past Lower Farm, take the track to the right and continue along this past several houses to Coathouse Farm, which stands alone in the fields.

## 9 SP359215

Turn right here, following the parish boundary hedge. The path here is very different to the grassy track of the Saltway. This little valley is below the spring line and the ground is much damper as the soil is clay rather than limestone. The grass has been taken over by tall, tussocky species which crowd out most of the flowering plants.

The path continues to a marshy area (where care or good footwear is necessary!) which has some interesting plants not often seen in the surrounding well-drained agricultural land.

Continue across a small stone bridge over Taston Brook. The steep banks provide a habitat for moisture- and sun-loving plants, a contrast to the shady damp area just walked through. Depending on the season, ragged robin, meadow sweet, water forget-me-not and marsh marigold can be seen.

The trail crosses diagonally left over the next field, an example of ridge-and-furrow which has remained undisturbed by ploughs since the Middle Ages.

## 10 SP355217

Looking back across the small valley to the south-east is the site of the deserted medieval village of Cote, whose presence is remembered in Coathouse Farm as well as several field names – Cote Coppice, Coate Grounds and Hovel Ground. It is said that the outlines of house platforms and holloways are clearly visible in dry weather. A local legend says that silver from Spelsbury Church was buried in Cote fields during the upheavals of the Reformation.

## 11 SP350217

The trail now reaches Spelsbury. Turn left, then right along the road, past the old water fountain. Note the commemorative plaque. The nearby church is worth a

Coldron Mill

Spelsbury almshouses

Dean Grove

detour as it contains memorials to many of the owners of the manor over the centuries. Take the Chadlington road, turning left about ten yards down an unmade road, which leads across the fields at the back of the churchyard.

## 12 SP345211

The track leads to Coldron Mill, which was a working mill for at least a thousand years. When it fell into disuse after the First World War, the grinding gear was taken to the London Science Museum, but was destroyed in bombing in the last war. The mill-pond and sluices are not accessible but on its way down the valley, the stream forms an attractive wet-land area. The line of blackthorns are covered in lichen, a good indication that there is little air pollution here.

## 13 SP344210

Keeping the wet area and the row of sloes to the left, the trail crosses a stile and small stream, passing through a small meadow. One plant of interest is lady's mantle with pleated leaves and green-yellow flowers.

The path leads straight on through a gate into a wood, where it turns left. This is Dean Grove, part of an area of woodland recorded in the Domesday Book. It is an area of mostly hazel coppice with a rich woodland flora, flowering in the spring. The ground can be wet.

## 14 SP343206

The trail leaves the wood and crosses a grassy field to a gate, and then diagonally left across the next to a wooden footbridge across Coldron Brook, the parish boundary at this point. Here the trail meets the Oxfordshire Way.

Notice the effect of grazing on the vegetation in the second field, where all the tall plants, except nettles and thistles which have in-built protection, have been eaten. The only common plants here are low-growing or creeping species.

## 15 SP344205

The trail and the Oxfordshire Way follow the same route back to Charlbury so look for the waymarks. The path skirts a patch of rough ground containing gorse with the appropriate field-name of Low Furze. This is probably a remnant of part of the old Common. The path then runs along the edge of woodland.

It then follows a hedge marking the end of several narrow fields which show signs of ridge-and-furrow, indicating that these fields were not extensively ploughed after enclosure but used for animals. Some of the hedges in this area may be three or four hundred years old, but were planted not formed from the remnants of cleared woodland.

The trail turns right on reaching Water Lane which tends to live up to its name, so an alternative route leaves the Lane by a stile on the left after a short distance and crosses a field.

The path joins the Charlbury – Spelsbury road, with Charlbury to the right. The Spendlove Centre is found by taking the second turning on the left in the town, while the station is sign-posted to the right.

Bbont Nature Reserve

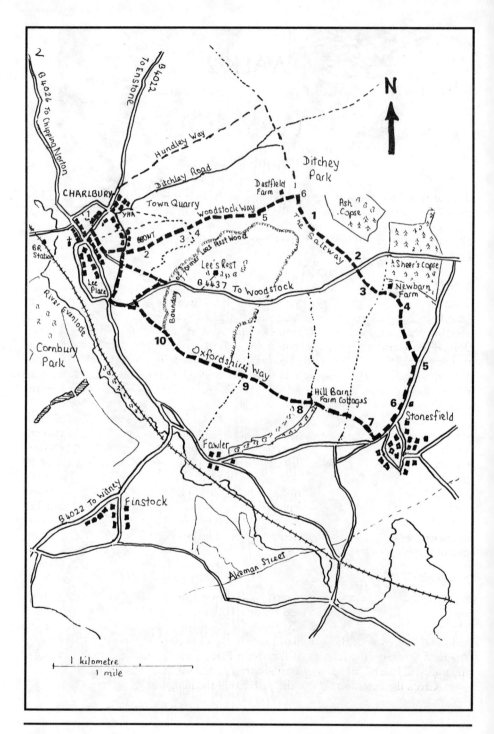

# WALK 2

# SALTWAY SOUTH

*6 miles (10 km)*

This walk is based on the southern portion of the Saltway, which can be reached by any of the three access routes described earlier. The trail leads to Stonesfield, a village which dates back to Roman times and has a recent industrial interest. The return to Charlbury is via part of the Oxfordshire Way which follows the old boundary of Lee's Rest Wood.

## 1 SP383197

Turning south at any of the access points (i.e. Dustfield Farm, Ditchley Gate or Hundley Way) the most interesting part of the Saltway soon becomes apparent. It widens out to a maximum of about seventy-five feet and contains a rich and varied flora. Two ancestors of modern cultivated vegetables occur here, wild parsnip, a tall yellow umbellifer which smells of parsnip when the stem is crushed and wild carrot, a white umbellifer often having a dark purple or black sterile flower in the centre of the flat flower head. This acts as a fly mimic and encourages flies to come to the flowers and so pollinate them.

These plants are present because the track has never been sprayed with pesticides or fertilizer and in fact, until a few years ago, was very overgrown with scrub. When this was cleared the original flora reappeared. To retain this rich flora the verges need to be managed by mowing or grazing, as they were in the past by the flocks of passing sheep, in order to prevent a further encroachment by scrub. The hedges are interesting examples of woodland relic flora with many shrub and herb species more commonly found in woodland such as dog's mercury, bluebell and yellow archangel. A specimen of wild service tree, which is usually only found in ancient woodland and infrequently at that, can be spotted in the hedge near the junction of the track with the B4437.

## 2 SP388192

Here the Saltway meets a more recent road, the turnpike of 1800 between Charlbury and Woodstock, which was based on one of the tracks through Lee's Rest Wood. On a map of 1797, the Saltway seems to split into two parts here, one route following the edge of the woodland which can be seen to the left and linking with Akeman Street on the far side of Blenheim Park, and the other following the route the trail will follow, meeting Akeman Street to the south of Stonesfield.

Cross the road and follow the path along the hedge.

## 3 SP390189

The hedge for part of its length forms a parish boundary between Fawler and Spelsbury. It follows a sinuous curve which usually indicates a boundary hedge and also contains a high number of species. The path passes over a stile near Newbarn Farm, which is shown on the map of 1797. Sheer's Copse, which lies behind the farm, is a remnant of Wychwood Forest, but is now a mixture of broad-leaved deciduous species and conifers.

## 4 SP393186

Going through two small fields, the trail continues along a track with an unspoilt verge and hedge on the right, whilst on the left you are likely to see intensively cultivated cereal crops. Cereals were developed from wild grasses native to the Middle East several thousands of years ago. Modern breeding has introduced several special characteristics. Notice the uniformity of the crop, all growing to the same height with large even-sized seeds ripening at the same time and compare this with wild grasses in the hedgerow. The cultivated seeds are difficult to remove from the seed head whereas wild grasses easily shed their seeds. This helps the farmer harvest the crop without wastage, the grain being removed during the threshing process.

The track becomes slightly muddy as it dips into the head of a small valley, near a spring, known as Ruddy Well, which provided part of the water supply for Stonesfield for many years. In 1897 water was piped from Ruddy Well to a village tap, paid for by public subscription. This tap can still be seen in the village along the trail.

## 5 SP395182

Turning right, the trail leads onto Stonesfield Riding, an old road, which from its name originally went through woodland. The field on the right is known as Gerner's Sart, 'sart' being a corruption of assart, meaning clearing of woodland. A perambulation of Wychwood dated 1298 records Gerner's Wood here and it is possible that this field dates from about this time.

Stonesfield has a long history with two Roman villas in the area. One was a small house situated near what is now the B4437, and the other near Akeman Street on the south-east of the village. It was discovered in 1712 and had four mosaic floors as well as baths and a central heating system or hypocaust. Unfortunately it was ploughed over soon afterwards, but some remains are in the Ashmolean Museum.

## 6 SP391173

Keep going straight on through the village, looking out for the village tap on the left about halfway down the hill.

Stonesfield was famous for its production of slates until the late nineteenth century. Although it has been described as originating in Roman times, there are no medieval records of the industry which was in operation by the seventeenth century. The slates were formed by the splitting action of frost on a particular type of limestone which occurs in spherical lumps called 'potlids'. It was mined and stored underground or in soil-covered clamps as it had to be kept damp until a suitable frost

Drinking fountain, Charlbury

The Saltway

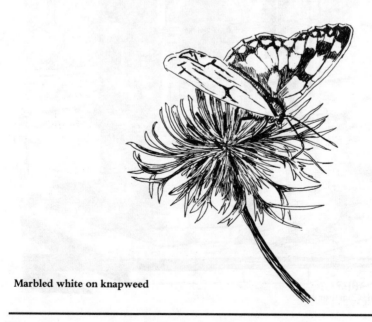

**Marbled white on knapweed**

occurred, when it was exposed and the slates were formed, splitting along the bedding plane of the stone. The 'diggers' were usually farm workers who, during the slacker winter months, dug for slate on a part-time basis. The 'slatters' were the men who shaped the slates and were more likely to work full time at this job. At one time Stonesfield had an almost lunar landscape because of the mounds of waste material lying about, used in the 1950s and '60s for road construction. The industry fell into disuse, the last pit closing in 1911, as Welsh slates, made from a different rock and by a different process, became cheaper and easier to obtain in the late nineteenth century.

Another unique feature of the Stonesfield geology is the abundance of fossils which can be found in the area. The limestone beds were laid down in shallow water conditions and a wide diversity of land and aquatic flora and fauna fossil remains have been identified. The site is world famous for vertebrate fossils with many remains of dinosaurs, marine crocodiles, pterosaurs and mammal-like reptiles. The first dinosaur ever to be recognized and described was found here in the early nineteenth century and there was a thriving cottage industry selling fossil remains to visitors, although the best specimens were kept for the university professors.

At the bottom of the hill, turn left up a stony track where the trail meets the Oxfordshire Way. Look back for a good view of Stonesfield, the old village a typical 'industrial' collection of closely-packed cottages compared to the later and modern arrangement with gardens.

## 7 SP384177

The trail leads straight on, through large arable fields, following the route of a well defined track between Charlbury and Stonesfield shown on the map of 1797 and defined as a Public Road on the Charlbury Tithe Award Map of 1847.

## 8 SP382177

The path bears left and starts to descend into a small valley near Hill Barn Farm Cottages. There is an area here of unimproved grassland with a good display of limestone flora. Look for thyme and marjoram with their purple flowers in July and August. The aromatic perfume of their leaves has led to their use as herbs in cooking. Stemless thistle occurs very close to the ground and the whole plant turns a golden brown in the autumn. Woolly thistle in contrast is a tall plant and can be identified by the spiral pattern on the unopened flowerheads. Further along the track is a patch of wild mignonette, an attractive plant with spikes of tiny pale green flowers.

The path then climbs again passing a thick hedge to the left, on the top of the hill. This is, in fact a double hedge, filled with undergrowth, presumably the remains of the old public road. There were several old slate mines in these fields but all trace of them has gone.

## 9 SP374181

A path to the left leads to Fawler, formerly a hamlet in Charlbury parish, where Roman remains were found in the nineteenth century. The path leading off to the right could therefore conceivably have linked the Fawler settlement with the one found at Lee's Rest to the north.

The Oxfordshire Way continues straight on. The track becomes hedged on both sides and within a short distance follows, on the right, the southern edge of the site of Lee's Rest Wood. It is fascinating to observe the hedge flora and see that the species which commonly indicate ancient woodland make an appearance as the old boundary of the wood, felled little over a hundred years ago, is reached, marked by a hedge. This unspoilt strip of woodland relic is rich in plant species and so provides food plants for insects and a safe habitat for birds.

## 10 SP364186

Gaps in the hedge to the left provide a wide viewpoint across to Cornbury Park, the last remaining large area of Wychwood Forest and also to Leafield on the skyline with a church steeple and a group of trees which stand on the top of a Bronze Age round barrow.

The trail meets the B4437 on the outskirts of Charlbury. The Spendlove Centre can be reached by turning left and then taking the right turn at the junction. Follow this road until the footpath opposite Blenheim Farmhouse is reached and retrace your steps via Willow Walk to the car park.

There is an alternative route found by turning right up the B4437 for a quarter of a mile and then following a path between two hedges which emerges on the road near the Slade where the walk began. If the station is required then take the middle road at the junction leading down to the town.

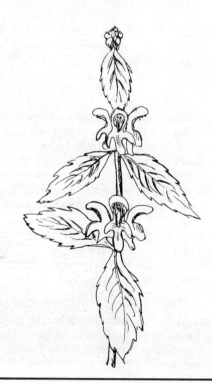

**Yellow archangel**

Church Street, Charlbury

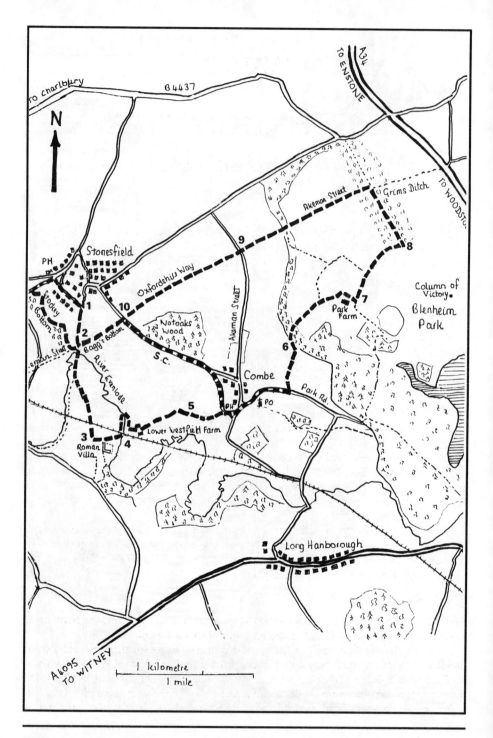

# WALK 3

# NORTH LEIGH VILLA, COMBE AND BLENHEIM PARK

*8 miles (13 km), or shorter walk of 3.5 miles (5.5km)*

This walk starts at Stonesfield, a village with a long and interesting industrial history (see Walk 2), passes the Roman villa at North Leigh, through Combe and crosses Blenheim Park before returning to Stonesfield via Akeman Street.

## 1 SP394169

The walk starts at the top of Brook Lane, an old path leading down from Stonesfield to the River Evenlode. It is stony in places and care should be taken. The antiquity of the path is shown by the height of the banks on each side, the path being worn down over the centuries. The flora reflects the unspoilt nature of the area, with plants indicative of old woodland, whilst in autumn look out for the silvery, fluffy heads of wild clematis (traveller's joy or old man's beard).

## 2 SP393164

Cross the river by the wooden footbridge. Looking back, you can see a series of terraces on the hill side which follows the route of Akeman Street, a demonstration of Roman expertise in civil engineering.

Carry straight on over the next field to the hedge, where the left fork should be taken. As you walk the field footpath, notice how the vegetation is mainly small grasses and low-growing plantains capable of withstanding moderate trampling where taller plants could not.

Follow this up the hill where it becomes a farm track and crosses the railway. Here the hedges are cut in a tapered 'A' shape, the broad base and the top regrowth intended to benefit small mammals, birds and insects. Continue to the sign for North Leigh Roman Villa and turn left here.

## 3 SP397155

The path carries on around the left-hand side of the villa site which is officially open from April to the end of October, when guide books are available.

The villa was first built in the second century, although there is evidence of pre-Roman settlement. It was a one storey, partly timber building which gradually evolved into a large elaborate house. Some of the stone used was hard Oolite quarried from nearby Sturt Wood and signs of a track linking the two are visible on aerial photos. It was occupied until the early fifth century, being most prosperous during the first half of the fourth century. The inhabitants would have been members of the British governing class, not Roman immigrants. Before excavation, the site was marked by the field name: Roman Piece. When excavation started in 1815, crowds of excited sightseers took souvenirs, destroying a mosaic pavement in the process.

## 4 SP399158

Follow the path to the river, left under the railway bridge where, immersed in the stream, the long flexible stems and threadlike leaves of water crowfoot can be seen, easily resisting the water flow. Carry on to a farm bridge and cross the river. Turn right and follow the path up the hill bearing left to Lower Westfield Farm.

Follow the farm road in front of the farmhouse and continue, climbing up the valley side. There is a good view here. The river has worn a wide valley in the softer limestone, leaving the harder rock to form the valley sides. The river moves relatively slowly here, following a meandering course marked by water-side trees like alder and willow, which has been pollarded in the past to provide a supply of willow poles and laths.

## 5 SP410158

The track leads to Combe past an area of young plantation and scrub which provides a good habitat for birds. In winter look out for mixed flocks with goldfinches, greenfinches, linnets, chaffinches and sparrows, feeding on teasle and dock seeds. Enter Combe and follow the road to the village centre, past the site of the old Pound.

*SHORT CUT Follow the road marked Stonesfield, passing Notoaks wood on the right and rejoining the trail guide at point 10 by turning left into Bagg's Bottom in a dip in the road.*

Combe was originally a settlement in the valley and was held by the Bishop of Bayeux at the time of the Domesday Book. By about 1350 the settlement had moved up to its present position on the hill top, and by the end of the century the church of St Laurence was built by the monks of Eynsham Abbey who held the manor. The church is worth a visit to see the remains of the original fifteenth-century wall paintings and a rare medieval stone pulpit. On the edge of the green is a notice board with more information.

Keep to the road on the right of the green, passing the lane to the church and the post office and continue along the road past the sports field. Notice two areas on the left, which were probably old ponds, indicated by the presence of willows. Past the end of the houses, there is a path signed to the left. Follow this across a field.

## 6 SP419165

The path reaches a wall and continues left for a short distance along it, before crossing a stile into Blenheim Park. Once over the wall, turn left for ten yards, then fork right down through the trees. Originally Woodstock deer park, Blenheim was landscaped by Capability Brown in the eighteenth century after coming into the ownership of the Dukes of Marlborough. Famed as a tourist attraction, the park is also a modern agricultural estate.

Stonesfield ford

**Long-tailed field mouse**

**Cowslips**

There is a mixture of trees in this area, with some old beech, younger sycamore and saplings of young hardwood trees, protected in their first few years from grazing damage by rabbits and deer by polythene tubes which also act as mini-greenhouses, encouraging a good start.

Follow the path signs crossing an estate track and climbing up through a scrubby patch to emerge at the edge of a cultivated field. After harvest, while the stubble remains, fields like this are good places to see pheasants feeding. Go left along the hedge and follow the path to a vehicle track alongside a conifer plantation with cotoneaster and grass planted for pheasant cover and food.

Continue to Park Farm, the site of one of the medieval park lodges. In the eighteenth century there was a menagerie there and, until the mid-nineteenth century, when the present large farm was built, the site was called the Dog Kennel, presumably because the duke's hounds were kept there.

## 7 SP425171

Just past Park Farm take the path to the left, crossing a cattle grid. Continue straight on along the side of the fence and skirting a clump of beech. Further on to the right is a group of horse chestnut trees. They have a clever way of showing bees which flowers to visit, those needing pollination having a yellow central spot, which then changes to pink when this has occurred, thus informing the bees not to waste time visiting pollinated flowers. The path veers to the right and carries on towards the main park road, edged on each side with a recently planted avenue of limes, replacing the elms lost in the dutch elm disease outbreak in the mid 70s. The stumps can still be seen and are good sites for soft fleshy tripe fungus. On cool sunny days in early spring or late autumn, the dark wood warms up and is used by flies for sunbathing to keep warm and active.

## 8 SP427183

The trail continues left along this road, with views of Blenheim Palace and the Column of Victory behind. After crossing one cattle grid, a second is reached, where the trail then turns left. At this point an extensive series of earthwork banks can be seen, dissected by the route of Akeman Street. This is Grim's Ditch, built in the Iron Age before the coming of the Romans, who based Akeman Street on an already existing track linking two powerful British tribes, the Dobunni in the Cirencester area and the Catuvellauni centred on St Albans.

Follow the path, now Akeman Street, over the fields and through a belt of trees to the park wall, which is crossed by a ladder stile.

## 9 SP412177

The trail continues on the route of Akeman Street along field edges to the Stonesfield – Combe road. On the way it crosses a lane and passes the parish boundary on the right, marked by a curving line between two fields. There are some small areas of unspoilt grassland along the path with cowslips and violets in the spring. Near the road, in the field to the right is the site of Stonesfield villa which dates from the fourth century. Mosaics and a hypocaust or hot air system were found in the eighteenth century, but were ploughed over soon afterwards. Some fragments of mosaic are in the Ashmolean Museum in Oxford.

## 10  SP399169

*Rejoin here if taking the short cut.*

After crossing the road, the path descends through a steep–sided valley, Bagg's Bottom. Immediately to the right, the patches of scrub in the field mark the site of some old Stonesfield slate quarries. The valley is a good habitat for a wide variety of wildlife with, in season, colourful areas of wet-land and limestone grassland as well as scrub, all of which provide food and shelter for many birds and insects. The valley is one of the best sites in West Oxfordshire for spotting tree pipits.

## 11  SP394165

After crossing a small stream and two stiles, the trail is back at the River Evenlode footbridge, having passed around the base of the terraces of Akeman Street.

To return to Stonesfield, you can either retrace your steps up Brook Lane, or else take the path a little further on to the right, through woodland along the edge of a steep–sided field. This is Stockey Bottom and is another area rich in wildlife. The planted woodland is dominated by beech, which is infrequent in this area. The path finishes on the road, where the trail turns right and returns to Stonesfield. Look out for an alleyway to the right which climbs past a cottage and emerges on the road at the top. Follow this to the right and keep going until the top of Brook Lane is reached and you are back at the start of the walk.

**Rock rose**

**Stockey Bottom**

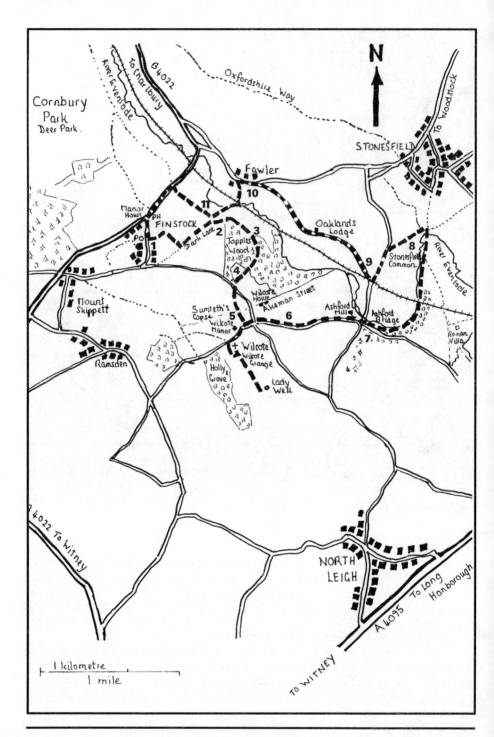

# WALK 4

# FINSTOCK, WILCOTE AND FAWLER

*8 miles (13 km)*

This walk passes through the site of a deserted medieval village, now covered in woodland, to Wilcote which dates back to Roman times, along the river Evenlode to Stonesfield Common and back to Finstock via Fawler. The route can be very muddy so good footwear is essential.

## 1 SP361165

At Finstock, park in School road, and take the track, Ward Lane, near the post office. The path passes the village allotments where a Roman terracotta lamp was found some years ago.

Where the path turns to the right over a stile, there are wide views over to Fawler with a pattern of regular rectangular fields showing that they date from the eighteenth-century enclosures. The path continues downhill, flanked on the left by a field called The Sarts, showing that it originated through woodland clearance.

Climb over another stile and turn left along a track, called locally Dark Lane, which originally went to a ford, known as Dunford, which led to Fawler. It was still in use in the nineteenth century. Accumulation of nutrients in the soil of the valley bottom has encouraged nettles, while thistles can survive in the poorer soil on the slopes. Although the field is grazed, both these plants survive due to their natural defences.

## 2 SP369166

The track bears to the right and becomes a sunken holloway, climbing up the valley slope. Along each side, woodland flora can be found, showing that this track evolved long ago when the surrounding area was covered in woodland. There are large coppiced hazel bushes and in February, when the male catkins are ripe and yellow, look for the tiny red tufts of the female flowers on large buds on the branches which will eventually give rise to the nuts.

As the track reaches the top of the hill, the woodland on the right is called Topples Wood. It varies in character, but here is a mixture of relatively recent conifer plantation with some tall standard ash trees. Ash timber is tough, elastic and light and acts as a shock-absorber when used as handles for garden tools, pickaxes, hammers and walking sticks.

**Wilcote Church**

**Avenue of pollarded ash**

Ashford Mill

## 3 SP374165

Further on, the track known as Topples Lane passes between conifer plantations followed by some areas of beech, now growing amongst the remnants of the conifers originally planted to 'nurse' them along and to protect them from extremes of wind and weather.

As the track continues, the wood changes in character again, becoming mixed deciduous. Here a mixture of coppiced hazel with tall standard oaks can be seen which was the old method of woodland management, used to ensure that there was a constant supply of small hazel wood for fires, fences and repairs as well as large oak timber for building. On the right, alongside the path, is an obviously old boundary bank used to demarcate areas of coppice woodland which were cut at different times. With the addition of a wooden fence, deer could be excluded to prevent them eating the new coppice growth.

Topples Wood marks the site of a medieval settlement, Tappewell, remembered in the former field names of Lower, Middle and Upper Topwell while Grant's Field recalls a thirteenth-century landlord, Robert Grant. Tappewell was once a hamlet of Charlbury, as was Finstock. In 1316 it belonged to the Abbey of Eynsham and had eight tenants paying fourteen shillings (70p) rent to the Abbey. It was mentioned in records up to 1524 with two houses on the site then, after which time it seems to have disappeared. The most likely site for the hamlet is near the holloway.

## 4 SP371159

After emerging from the wood, the track crosses the open Upper Topwell Field with some fine examples of spreading oak trees, a contrast to those seen in the wood which were tall and slender due to the proximity of other trees. On the left is a view over to Wilcote House, which will be passed later along the trail. The track reaches a road. Turn left and after a few yards a path leads off to the right, diagonally over a field. The route of the Roman Akeman Street crosses this field, level with the edge of the wood, Sumteth's Copse, at the top of the slope.

## 5 SP372154

The path emerges on the road next to seventeenth-century Wilcote Manor. Wilcote dates back at least to Roman times, when there was a settlement here. In 1086, Wilcote was a large cleared area in Wychwood Forest, but later during the Middle Ages the settlement contracted. Wilcote House, built in the time of Elizabeth I but modernized in the nineteenth century, may be seen further along the trail.

*To the right a diversion of about a mile leads to Wilcote Grange and church and to a series of medieval fishponds.*

Follow the road past the little church of St Peter and turn left at the side of the farm buildings. Take the path to the right of the pond and then bear to the left of the dead elm tree. Keep on the track as it bears right and follow it downhill through an avenue of ancient pollarded ash, so old that most of the trees are hollow and in some cases split in two. At the bottom of the track is an old walled well, known as Lady Well, reputed to be an ancient fertility spring, and which used to be visited by local people on Lady Day (25 March). Beyond this is an overgrown wet area with a series

**Comfrey**

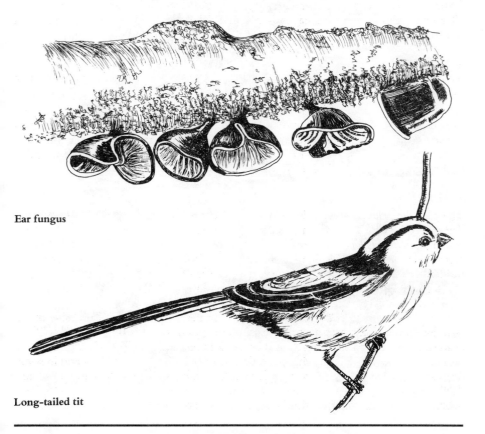

**Ear fungus**

**Long-tailed tit**

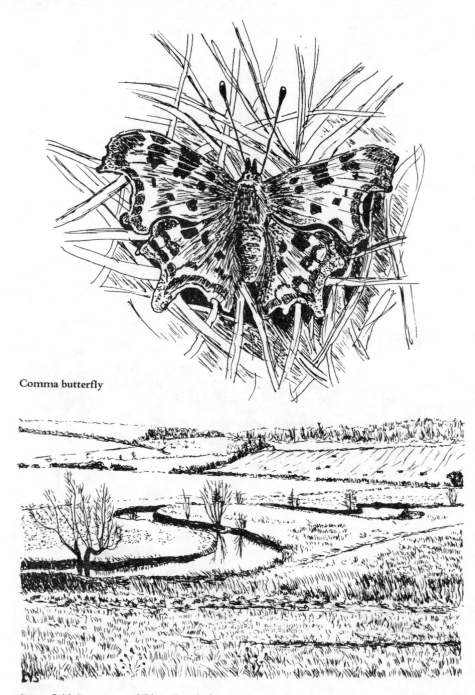

**Comma butterfly**

**Stonesfield Common and River Evenlode**

of ponds leading from one to another for the provision of fish for food in the Middle Ages. Look out for the huge stems of giant hogweed, standing about twelve feet tall. This plant can cause a severe skin irritation so don't touch.

*Retrace your steps to return to the main part of the trail.*

Past Wilcote Manor keep straight on over the crossroads, although a good view of Wilcote House can be seen just a few yards to the left. In the field to the right the bumps show the remains of the settlement.

## 6  SP380155

The road continues downhill with views ahead over to Stonesfield and the Evenlode valley. On the dry stone walls, mosses and lichens grow. Lichens are intimate associations of fungi and algae, and can tolerate exposed harsh conditions. They can take many forms, but here they resemble a white covering of cement. Moss tends to be more dependent on water and nutrients. Notice how they tend to be found on the shadier, sheltered sides and crevices of the walls.

At the bottom of the hill go straight on over the cross roads, to the left is Ashford Mill, a nineteenth-century corn mill built over the river. Here the banks are lined with moisture-loving willow and alder trees, and burr-reed, with its unusual balls of spiky flowers, flourishes at the water's edge.

## 7  SP388154

Just over the crossroads, there is a carpark to the left, with a footpath leaving in one corner. Take this path and follow it along the river valley. It can be rather slippery along this stretch so care is needed in places.

This is a shady damp area of woodland and scrub. Mosses grow up many of the tree trunks and notice that they are different types to those on the walls earlier. The flowers growing here indicate wet ground; meadow sweet, comfrey and great willow herb are all lovers of damp places. Look out for various types of fungi, especially in the autumn. Woodland and riverside birds such as warblers and kingfishers may be glimpsed or heard and, in the winter, groups of pinkish long-tailed tits may be spotted.

Further along as the path reaches fields, there is a large area of nettles, which although unfriendly to humans is a good source of food for many caterpillars of peacock, small tortoishell, red admiral and comma butterflies. Amongst the nettles are tall hemlocks, a very poisonous plant, with feathery leaves and purple blotches on the stems.

## 8  SP392161

Follow the path to the river and cross by the footbridge. Turn left and climb between steep banks up on to Stonesfield Common. These banks mark a section of Akeman Street and interesting plants grow there. Mullein can be recognized by its velvety leaves and tall spike of yellow flowers while dog's mercury, a woodland plant, is the first plant to emerge in the spring and one of the last to die back in winter, thus making the most use of times when the tree cover is least.

Stonesfield Common is one of only two areas of common left in this part of Oxfordshire and has a rich flora with a colourful display of summer flowers.

Traditionally the common was sheep-grazed, and this sort of management is necessary to retain the flowering plants, which otherwise will be crowded out by ranker vegetation. Looking at the winding river valley, the uniform agricultural land can be compared with the flower-rich natural grassland of the Common.

The trail crosses the top of the Common and emerges on to the road. Turn left.

## 9 SP386160

At the road junction take the road to the right and continue towards Fawler. Along the road, Topples Wood can be seen across the valley beyond the railway, which was built in 1853 as part of the line to Worcester. Some of the roadside verges have limestone flora, so look out for flowers and butterflies in the summer. One unusual plant is goldilocks, a buttercup whose small flowers often have petals missing and is more normally associated with ancient woodland.

Near Oaklands Lodge, an isolated house on the right, a Roman farm site has been found, one of several in this area.

## 10 SP372170

At Fawler, take the first turning to the left and follow the path across the field to the railway bridge. At this point care and common sense are needed, as the path climbs up the right hand side of the bridge and crosses the track to descend on the left of the bridge on the other side, thus crossing both the river and the railway. Keeping the river on your right-hand side, follow the path until it leaves the river bank and crosses a stile into a field.

## 11 SP369167

Follow the line of the valley up to a stile and then either keep straight on to return to Finstock via Dark Lane, or take the path to the right.

This path enters a field, and crosses it to reach a track leading to the road, where you turn left. The lower slopes of the field were known as Longmeade when they were enclosed by Eynsham Abbey in 1363. The hedge bordering the road has seven species per thirty yard stretch and is likely to date from this time. In contrast, many other hedges around Finstock fields were planted following their enclosure in 1860, when the land was owned by Lord Churchill of Cornbury Park.

The road was an old track known as Stoney Way in the thirteenth century linking Finstock and Charlbury. Between 1798 and 1800 the road was improved and made into a turnpike, which meant that users paid a toll to help maintain the road.

When the seventeenth-century Finstock Manor House is reached, turn left past The Crown to return to your starting point.

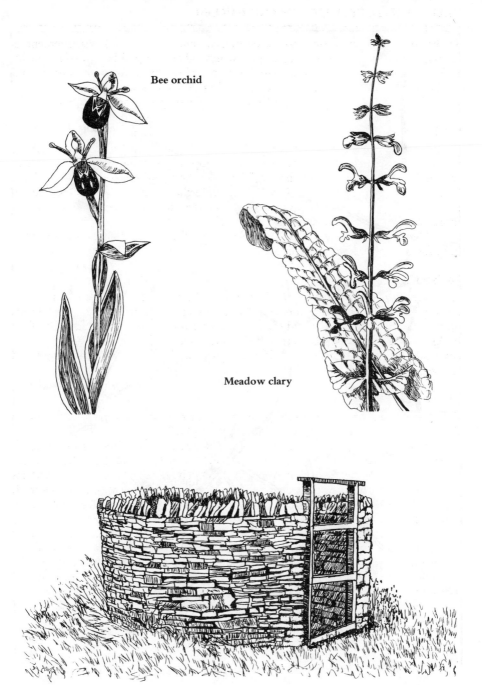

Bee orchid

Meadow clary

Lady well

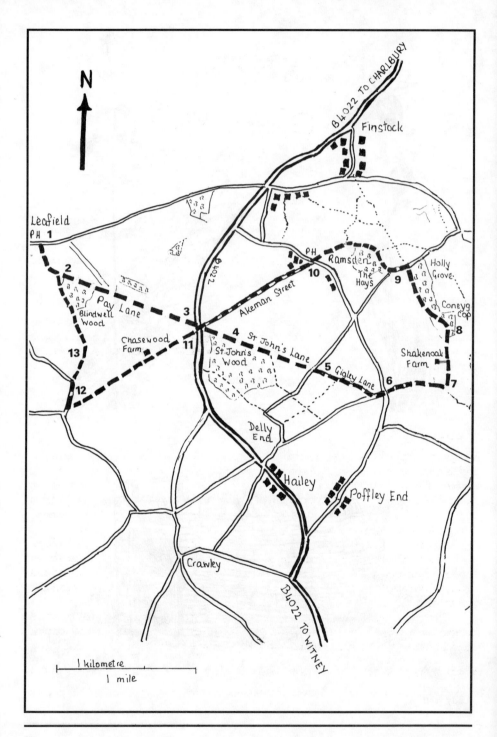

N

Leafield
PH **1**

**2**

Pay Lane

Blindwell
Wood

**13**

Chasewood
Farm **11**

St John's
Wood

**12**

**3**

**4** St John's Lane

**5** Gigley Lane **6**

**7**

Akeman Street

B4022

PH
Ramsden
The
Hays

**10**

**9**

Holly
Grove

Coneyg
Cop

**8**

Shakenoak
Farm

Delly
End

Hailey

Poffley End

Crawley

B4022 TO CHARLBURY

Finstock

B4022 TO WITNEY

1 kilometre
1 mile

# WALK 5

# LEAFIELD, SHAKENOAK AND RAMSDEN

*8 miles (13 km), or the shorter walk of 4 miles (6.5 km)*

This walk starts at Leafield and follows a figure-of-eight course which means it can be shortened. It uses several ancient tracks and crosses the site of an important Roman villa. Parts of this walk can be rather muddy so waterproof footwear is advisable.

## 1 SP325155

Parking in Leafield, head for the Spindle Tree public house at the Finstock end of the village and just past this take the lane to the right. This lane is walled on each side and shows a rich display of mosses and lichens, most of which only thrive in a clean atmosphere, so obviously here the air is free from much industrial pollution. See how many different types you can distinguish. Feel the different textures of the lichens but be careful not to damage them.

Continue to a fork near some houses and bear left.

## 2 SP330150

This track is called Pay Lane; it continues for two miles in a more or less straight line and is thought possibly to be Roman in origin. It is mentioned in an Anglo-Saxon charter of Witney dated 969 in conjunction with another track which you will see at the end of this walk. The two tracks meeting at the fork you have just passed form two sides of a triangle, which was called 'cygnes steorte' in Old English, meaning 'King's pointed piece of land'.

On the right, Blindwell Wood is soon reached, an area of ancient woodland with many species needing long undisturbed conditions in order to flourish. In spring, primroses, wood anemone and yellow archangel demonstrate the woodland origin of most of the track. This is all that remains of a large area of woodland shown on both sides of the track on a map of 1797.

Further along the lane you will notice, on the right, a high wire fence which encloses deer farmed for venison. The path becomes more overgrown and can be muddy. In fact this was recorded as a marshy clearing in the Witney Charter.

## 3 SP344145

When you reach the road, cross straight over and keep following the line of the track.

*SHORT CUT If you want a shorter walk turn right for a short distance past the farmhouse and take a path to the right at the back of some farm buildings. Follow the guide from point 11.*

## 4 SP347143

This is St John's Lane, carrying on from Pay Lane. You will see some interesting plants, including one that looks rather like the familiar garden laurel. This smaller, less obvious plant is spurge laurel and is one that indicates a long continuity of woodland. In fact, St John's Wood is a substantial remnant of Wychwood forest and this track is referred to as Hunter's Way in a 1044 charter and was recorded as the northern boundary of this segment of the Forest in 1300. The bluebells and primroses will continue to flourish as long as the tree canopy does not become too thick. The old method of coppicing the woodland in rotation over a period of years had the benefit of thinning the canopy so that these species had enough light to thrive. The path can be very muddy along its length.

## 5 SP357140

When the path reaches the road, carry on more or less straight across the junction and follow Gigley Lane. Notice the striking row of holly trees, growing in a typical conical shape, aided no doubt by Christmas pruning! Mistle thrushes also appreciate the berries, which are not damaged by frost, standing guard over chosen trees to ensure a winter supply of food. They may be seen in nearby fields.

At the junction turn left and then, at the main road, find the track slightly to the left across the road.

## 6 SP370139

Take this track, keeping to the right at a small junction. After this, notice the bank in the hedge on the left, which marks the parish boundary between North Leigh and Hailey. These village names indicate the once wooded nature of this area, both having their roots in the word 'leah' meaning a clearing or open space in a wood. If you have an Ordnance Survey map notice how many others there are in the Wychwood area.

## 7 SP372138

Look out for a footpath sign to the left and follow this path along a hedge, first on the right and then on the left-hand side. These fields were the site of human occupation from at least the Bronze Age, through the Iron Age up to the Saxon period around 750. A villa was built here and was most prosperous during the second century. As nearby North Leigh villa became more important, so Shakenoak contracted, although Germanic mercenaries were stationed there in the fifth century, brought in by the Romans to strengthen their declining defences. By the seventh century there was probably a Saxon village here, the mercenaries opening the way for the related Saxon incomers.

Follow the path until it reaches a wood. Turn right along the wood edge for a short distance, then turn left into the wood, taking a well defined path.

## 8 SP372145

This wood is called Coneygar Copse and hidden in the undergrowth are some pillow mounds made in the early Middle Ages for keeping rabbits, as the name 'coney' suggests. Rabbits are not native to Britain but were introduced by the Normans. Originally they were unused to digging burrows and needed nurturing, so man-made burrows were provided. Notice the lack of young saplings in this woodland, possibly thinned in past management. White stitchwort carpets the edge of the path. This delicate plant was used as a cure for pains in the side, i.e. stitch.

The path continues along a woodland edge, having entered Holly Grove. This relatively small area of woodland is likely to be the one referred to in the Domesday Book entry for Wilcote as the dimensions are the same and it is obviously a very old wood with a rich flora and fauna. The wood is situated at the edge of the parish of North Leigh, parish edges being a common setting for woodland, and the remains of the parish boundary bank can be seen on your left.

## 9 SP365151

When you reach the road, turn left past a rough area which is a disused quarry, then take a path to the right along the edge of a wood. Its name, The Hayes, may indicate that in Medieval times it was a place from which deer were excluded. In autumn look out for parasol and puffball fungi. This wood also has a boundary bank, on top of which can be seen old remnants of coppiced hazel. In contrast to Coneygar Copse, notice the numerous saplings of ash, hazel and other trees.

The path skirts the top of the wood and, just before reaching a lane, passes a small pond with water-loving plants growing around the edge, forget-me-not, willow herb and brooklime.

Take the lane down to Ramsden.

## 10 SP357152

At the crossroads near the Royal Oak take the road straight ahead, past the church. This road is Akeman Street and its route will be followed for two miles. Walk along the road back to the junction with Pay Lane, St John's Lane and the B4022.

## 11 SP343145

At this junction, turn left along the road for a short distance then, just past the farm house, look for a path to the right, between stone walls. Take this and continue straight on, along the edge of the field, where the raised hump, or agger, of the Roman road can clearly be seen. The trail passes Chasewood Farm, a nineteenth-century model farm built by the Duke of Marlborough.

Now, the landscape becomes wide and open with good views to the south over Witney. This area, part of Wychwood Forest, was known as Witney Chase after 1294 when Edward I gave the hunting rights to the Bishop of Winchester, who owned land in the area. It was wooded up to the early nineteenth century.

During the Second World War this open land was used as an airfield, one of many in the Cotswolds, and reminders of this can be seen round about. Crossbred angora/cashmere goats, valuable for their wool, can sometimes be seen grazing here.

## 12 SP329136

The path continues over the grassland until it reaches a short track which leads down to the road. A large patch of old tarmac remains here. See how it is being colonized by thick carpets of moss which can cope with the lack of soil. As the moss decays it builds up a layer of humus, which will eventually form a soil layer. The moss is often scratched up by birds searching for food. In winter look out for birds, particularly redwings and fieldfares, Scandinavian migrants, feeding on berries in the tall hedge to the right.

On the road turn right. In autumn look for spindle trees with their pink fruits which open to reveal bright orange seeds, eaten by robins and other birds. As you walk, look up to the right where remains of gun emplacements from the Second World War can be seen in several places along this part of the walk.

The road makes a sharp left turn, but here go straight on along a grassy track.

## 13 SP330141

This is the other track mentioned in the Witney Charter which marked the boundary of the Bishop of Winchester's Witney estate, hence its name of Bishop's Way; it forms the other side of the pointed piece of land mentioned earlier. In contrast to Pay Lane it follows a curving route more typical of a boundary and is, in fact, still the parish boundary between Leafield and Crawley.

There is a pleasant view up the valley along the track. Most of the walls are overgrown with scrub and the path is rather bumpy in places where scrub has been cleared.

Continue back to the start of the walk in Leafield.

**Wood anemone**

**Parasol fungus**

**Redwing**

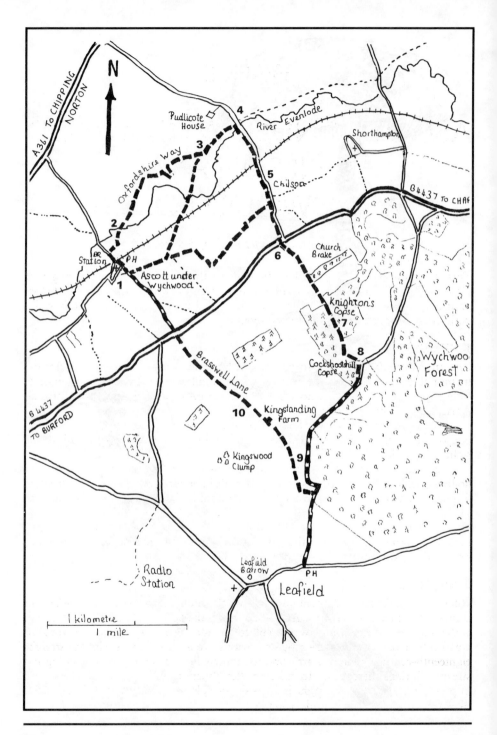

# WALK 6

# ASCOTT-UNDER-WYCHWOOD CHILSON AND WYCHWOOD FOREST

*6.5 miles (11 km), or shorter walk of 3.5 miles (5.5 km)*

This walk follows the Oxfordshire Way along the Evenlode valley, leaving it at Chilson and climbing up to walk through part of Wychwood Forest, before returning to Ascott-under-Wychwood. The going is good for most of this walk, with many open viewpoints of this unspoilt area.

## 1 SP302187

Park in Ascott, which can also be reached by train (very infrequent). Notice the memorial plaques around the tree on the triangular green. They commemorate sixteen women of Ascott, who were sent to prison in 1873 for trying to form an Agricultural Workers Union.

Make your way over the level crossing out of the village. On your right look out for a recently-made pond, fringed with reed-mace and take the footpath to the right just past it.

In the next two fields, there are extensive earthworks with bumps and hollows, which are the remains of a castle built in about 1130, during the turbulent dispute for the throne between Stephen and Matilda. It was demolished soon after 1175.

As the path bears to the left, look for the granary in the group of farm buildings to the right, around the old Manor House. It stands on staddle stones to protect the grain from rising damp and rodents.

## 2 SP301192

After crossing the river, the trail now follows the route of the Oxfordshire Way and is marked with yellow arrows. As you approach the far end of the large field, look at the thick hedge stretching away uphill to the left. This is an excellent example of a parish boundary hedge shown by its obvious age in comparison with the straight eighteenth-century hedges nearby and its sinuous line coinciding with a spring-fed stream. Springs here tend to arise at the junction of porous limestone and impermeable clay. On the right is a good example of an old pollarded oak. Such trees were often used as boundary markers.

**Half-timbered granary**

**Pollarded willows**

**Footbridge to Ascott Mill**

## 3 SP311200

*SHORT CUT A path to the right leads down to the river, crossing by a footbridge and passing eighteenth-century Ascott Mill, now disused, with remains of sluice and mill race visible. Follow this path back to Ascott.*

After crossing the next field, there is another area of bumps and hollows. This is the site of a medieval settlement, likely to be Pudlicote, which in 1279 had eight villeins and nine freemen. The land belonged to the Abbey of Eynsham and was deserted by 1334. From the air, the pattern of the buildings and tracks can clearly be seen.

Through the next gateway, the path enters a landscape of a later age, as it crosses the parkland of Pudlicote House. It is separated from the open grass by a ha-ha, a walled ditch, giving the occupants an impression of spaciousness, while keeping animals from the immediate area of the house. The large oaks were probably planted when the park was made during the eighteenth century.

## 4 SP315204

The trail now reaches a road, where it leaves the Oxfordshire Way. Before turning right over the river, have a look at the massive pollarded poplars on each side of the road to the left. Their tops are cut off every few years, which produces this characteristic tree-shape. A thoughtful owner has planted replacements alongside.

Follow the road up the hill to Chilson, but stop and look behind at the view of Pudlicote. The fields along the river bank share the name Ham, meaning waterside meadows. They are now improved grazing land.

The wide verges of this road show that it was made during the enclosure of the open fields. In summer, look in the hedges for purple flowers with spiky yellow centres, which closely resemble those of potato and tomato. This is woody nightshade and in fact these three plants are closely related. In autumn, the clusters of shiny red berries are quickly eaten by birds.

## 5 SP319194

*At Chilson you could return to Ascott-under-Wychwood by turning right 150 yards past Chilson Farm and following the Oxfordshire Way along the hillside above the south side of the river. This path enters the eastern edge of the village known as Ascott d'Oyley at Yew Tree Farm.*

Chilson is another village with its roots going back to Roman times as a villa site has been discovered here, linked by a road to Akeman Street to the south. Here major changes in the use of buildings are apparent as disused barns, built to store grain, are being converted into houses.

The road climbs up the hill out of Chilson and when it reaches a junction with the B4437, Charlbury to Burford road, turn right for a short distance before taking the lane to the left marked Chilson Hill.

## 6 SP323186

The footpath passes beside a cottage and then follows a hedge, crossing fields which were wooded in the early part of the nineteenth century. The view behind is over the

Pudlicote House

Avenue of poplars

Parish boundary pollarded oak

earlier part of the walk along the river valley. Look for the parish boundary hedge winding down the valley side, contrasting with the regular pattern of Parliamentary Enclosure fields, and the open parkland around Pudlicote House.

An open ride is reached, bordered by a strip of woodland called Church Brake. Pheasants and hares can be seen in the vicinity and it is worth approaching quietly to surprise them. The path continues straight on and enters Knighton's Copse, passing some disused gravel pits. The copse consists of natural broad-leaved woodland on the left with non-native, planted conifers on the right. Compare the difference in the two areas with much ground vegetation under the deciduous trees and hardly any in the coniferous part, as there is not enough light for plants to flourish and the fallen conifer needles acidify the soil.

The path becomes a wide grassy track and there is enough light here for some flowering plants to grow. The clover-shaped leaflets of wood sorrel and glossy leaves of bugle, both typical woodland plants, may be found here throughout the year.

## 7 SP326181

The path meets another at right angles. Turn left for a few metres and then right. The tall spreading conifers are scots pine which are native to Britain and can be identified by the orange bark near the top of the tree. Bracken covers the ground and in summer it forms a dense mass spreading by underground rhizomes or stems, making it hard to control. It is poisonous to animals so tends to spread unchecked. It grows in acid soils, so here the limestone must be deep beneath a cap of sand and gravel.

There is also a large patch of rosebay willow herb, a tall plant with pink-purple flowers in August and fluffy seeds later on. It grows in places where the earth has been disturbed or burnt, and is often seen on waste ground in towns, blown in on the wind. During the war it became abundant on bombsites, so living up to its North American name of fireweed.

The path continues, with a field on the left and the woods to the right. Bear left at a junction and look out for a bank in the woods on your right. This probably marks the line of an old track, Cockshoot Riding, which is shown in a map dated 1797. Continue to the road.

## 8 SP329177

Turn right and follow the road for some distance. The woodland on your left is the major part of Wychwood Forest which still remains. The bank at its edge contains a mixed collection of plants, some, such as wood spurge and dog's mercury, preferring a shady, woodland habitat and others, like rock-rose, which favour a limestone soil and sunshine. There are remnants of stone walls on the road sides providing a site for mosses and ferns.

To the right is High Lodge, a moated building once used as a hunting lodge. More flowering plants can be seen on the right verge, with yellow St John's wort, purple basil and knapweed and tall felty-leaved mullein. Along the wire fence shrubs are starting to appear, growing from seeds dropped by birds perching there.

As the road bends to the left there is a wide view to Leafield with, from right to left, a Bronze Age barrow topped with trees, a radio mast and the spire of the nineteenth-century parish church, designed by Sir Gilbert Scott in a gothic revival style.

## 9 SP324163

The road bends again and descends to a valley. In this vicinity there were several quarries producing forest marble, a particularly hard limestone suitable for sculpture. It was used for the chimney pieces in Cornbury House and also for the pillars and porticos of St John's College in Oxford. This part of the forest is a National Nature Reserve, but there is no public access except on Palm Sunday.

Opposite a gate into the woods, follow a track to the right leading to Kingstanding Farm. All these large fields were once King's Wood, part of Wychwood Forest belonging to the Crown until just over a hundred years ago, when the whole area was cleared and made into agricultural land. The farm was built at about the same time. Look for the date on the buildings. It is said that this place was where the King and his attendants would stand when hunting in the forest and the deer would be driven towards them. Over to the left is a group of trees known as Kingswood Clump, standing on a mound thought to be a round barrow. This is all that remains of King's Wood.

Continue along the track past the farm.

## 10 SP314174

The lane is known as Brasswell Lane and once led into the forest at Brasswell Gate. It is a good vantage point for a view of the Evenlode Valley, where the river makes a sudden change of direction when the underlying rock formation changes.

Continue downhill to cross the B4437 again. Just as you return to Ascott-under-Wychwood look out for a field on the left, just past the houses, where more bumps and hollows indicate that the village was once larger than it is now or else its focus has changed over the centuries. You are now back at your starting point.

Ferns on drystone wall

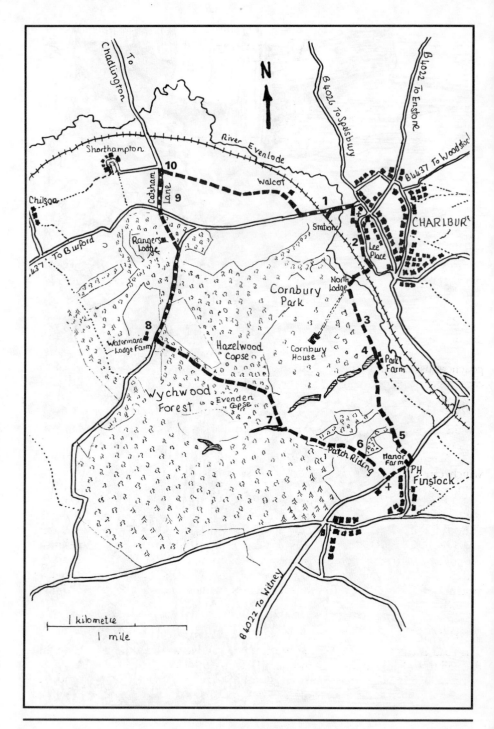

# WALK 7

# CORNBURY PARK AND WYCHWOOD FOREST

*8 miles (13 km)*

This walk passes through three distinct types of landscape, parkland, woodland and river valley, with panoramic views over the surrounding countryside. Part of the walk follows an ancient track through Wychwood Forest, which was reinstated as a footpath in December 1988. This area is a nationally important nature reserve, so please stay on the path and keep dogs on leads along this stretch of the route. It is muddy in places so good footwear is advisable.

## 1 SP353195

Starting at the station in Charlbury, cross over the river towards the town. Take the first turn to the right leading past the church. An old story says that local deer poachers used to hide their venison in some of the graves. Turn right out of the church yard and follow this road.

## 2 SP357190

On the right there is a good view of Cornbury Park with a classic parkland mixture of grassland and trees.

A little further along, on the left, is a wall with large clipped yews through which can be glimpsed Lee Place, a house dating in part from the seventeenth century or earlier, and named after the Lee family of Ditchley who owned it for a time in the eighteenth century. Its present owner is the Duke of Marlborough.

Turn right opposite the lodge gates to cross the railway and the river. Note the little well in the field on the left with a mushroom-shaped tiled roof. The tall trees along the river to the left are alder which can be identified by their dark red catkins in the spring and their small cone shaped fruit in autumn. Alders like wet conditions and their water-resistant wood was used for clogs and broomheads. Their huge root systems are favoured by otters for their dens or holts, but none have been seen here for many years.

## 3 SP355188

The road enters Cornbury Park at North Lodge and leads to Cornbury House, but the trail turns left here through the painted door on the left.

Cornbury originated as a royal hunting lodge in Wychwood Forest and was normally granted to the Ranger of the Forest. A hunting lodge was built by 1337 and the park was walled in 1383. Part of the mansion dates from about 1495, and the rest from 1631 when it was enlarged for the Earl of Danby. The park was disafforested in 1642 and so was no longer part of the Royal Forest and out of the jurisdiction of the Forest Laws. The Duke of Marlborough bought the Park in 1751 but it has changed hands several times since.

The path follows the tall deer fence along the side of the park, which has a typical landscape of large old pollarded trees, mostly oak with some horse chestnut. Several herds of fallow and sika deer roam the park. Only the males have antlers, those of the fallows being blade-like while those of the sikas are tall and branching.

## 4 SP358180

As the path approaches Park Farm look out on the right for an igloo-shaped building in the park. This is an ice house, which stored ice collected in the winter, for use throughout the summer. Nearby are remains of a Bronze Age round barrow and earthworks, one of many prehistoric sites in Cornbury and Wychwood.

The trail passes along the dam forming the lowest of a series of seven artificial lakes, originally built as three fishponds in Wychwood. Henry VIII is recorded as having ordered the Cornbury ponds to be stocked with carp. Now they provide a habitat for water plants and birds and if you are very lucky you may see a kingfisher.

Take a track to the right opposite the farm cottages, leading between paddocks and then bear left along a broad grassy avenue. Look back for a good view of Cornbury House.

## 5 SP358174

Go straight over at a junction of tracks and then bear left along a narrower track, which for part of its length is edged on the right with a small copse of hazel. The track bends and crosses a small steep valley, the sides of which have been left unploughed for many years. This provides cover for pheasants but also links several small pieces of woodland and therefore benefits all types of wildlife. The soil here is a good example of corn-brash, the rubbly limestone which got its name from the corn which thrives in the well-drained conditions.

The track reaches a group of old farm buildings around a grassy yard. The tall three-storey house is Manor Farm dating back to 1660. Look for the unusual oval windows on the top storey, with one set on its side.

Climb over the stone stile and turn right along the road. Walk with care as the traffic is fast here. Continue straight on along the road, past a lay-by until a track turns off to the right. Opposite is the church surrounded by many evergreen trees. The custom of planting yews in church yards is thought to date back to Roman times when it was used as a substitute for cypress to decorate graves.

## 6 SP358168

The track is called Patch Riding and leads into Wychwood Forest. Look for fossils in the stone walls to the right. These are remains of shellfish preserved in the marine deposits which formed the rock millions of years ago when this area was covered by a shallow sea. In spring, primroses can be found along this bank, a reminder that this area was once wooded. Further on you can find another woodland indicator, wood

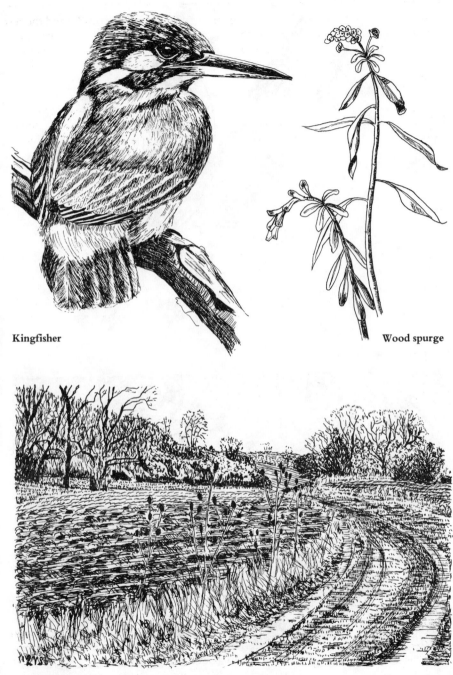

Kingfisher

Wood spurge

Patch Riding

**Great spotted woodpecker**

**Fungus growing on tree**

spurge, a plant attractive all year round, with dark green leaves on a reddish stem and greenish flowers early in spring later forming brown seeds which can lie dormant for a hundred and twenty-five years.

The track starts to descend and passes another area of hazel coppice, this time interspersed with tall standard oaks. Follow the sign to the left over a stile and carry on downhill between banks with primroses and foxgloves. Look for narrow deer tracks emerging from the undergrowth. At the bottom of the hill is a group of laurel bushes. Crushed laurel leaves release prussic acid and were used by Victorian insect collectors in their jars to kill their specimens.

The clean, spring-fed lake in the valley bottom is of national importance, supporting a rich variety of aquatic wildlife.

## 7 SP348172

The trail then bears right and climbs uphill past a saw mill, then emerges on an open grassy area with a wall beyond, which is the boundary of Cornbury Park. Follow the signs, leaving the track and crossing the grass taking the second left to walk up a broad ride.

Notice the large amount of fallen dead timber in this area. The rotting wood is good for numerous insects and fungi, which in turn are a food supply for birds and small mammals. Here there is not much evidence of regeneration of the trees by seedlings, which are probably damaged by deer or squirrels, although further along in the woods, there are numerous sycamore saplings.

Continue straight on along this track which becomes quite muddy. On each side there are banks marking the different copses in the Forest. By tradition there were eighteen copses throughout the forest, one of which was cut each year. The banks were used as bases for strong fences which were kept in place for eight years after cutting, to exclude deer and cattle. Hazlewood Copse on the right has remnants of old coppice stools, while on the left standard oaks and ash predominate.

Look out for several very large beech trees, one with an impressive display of bracket fungus. These trees are probably about three hundred years old and a rough estimation of the age can be found by measuring the girth at chest height. One inch represents approximately one year of age. Along this path you will see several typical woodland plants including early purple orchids, with their blotchy leaves growing early in the spring. Take care not to trample plants growing on the path.

## 8 SP332181

The path now reaches the road. Climb over the stile and turn right, continuing along the road for about a mile (2 km). To the left is an open area with a house and farm buildings. This is Ranger's Lodge, where there has been a large clearing for several hundred years, part of which was a sheep walk where flocks belonging to Shorthampton villagers had grazing rights.

At the junction take the road signed Chadlington. Along this short stretch of road, a row of mountain ash or rowan has been planted, which will grow to provide useful berries for birds.

Just before the next junction there is an opportunity to pause and look at the view, much of which covers the second half of the Saltway North Walk (1). From right to left, on the skyline the line of trees is Shilcott Wood, with the hamlet of Taston just visible behind the tower of Spelsbury church; the square of woodland in the valley is Dean Grove. An uncultivated rectangular patch on the hillside across the valley further to the left is Knollbury Camp, thought to date from the Iron Age.

## 9  SP333195

Cross the road, Catsham Lane, and continue straight on downhill. The verges here are worth looking at, as they contain a good variety of limestone grassland plants. One that is found here is autumn gentian, flowering in late August and September with pale purple spikes of flowers. Another interesting plant is the pink vetch-like sainfoin, which used to be grown for hay and to improve the soil fertility as it has the ability to add nitrogen to the soil.

## 10  SP334200

Continue downhill until a track leads off to the right, marked Oxfordshire Way.

A short diversion to Shorthampton can be taken here by carrying on a little further and taking the lane to the left. This hamlet has shrunk over the years and traces of the original extent of the village can be seen as earthworks in a field near the river. The Norman church has remains of medieval wallpaintings.

## 11  SP346198

The Oxfordshire Way is followed back to Charlbury. The path dips down to a hedge, which forms part of the parish boundary between Chilson and Charlbury. Look at the dead trees near the path. Those with flanges or wings along their branches are elm, which can also be identified when in leaf by the coarse texture of the leaves. Along the hedgerow in spring are the arrow-shaped leaves of lords-and-ladies, followed by the greenish flower sheath and in autumn you will see bright orange spikes of berries, which are poisonous.

Along this stretch of the walk there is a good view of the Evenlode valley. Note the irregularly sized fields across the river. These were enclosed in the seventeenth and eighteenth centuries by agreement between landowners, rather than by an Act of Parliament, which usually produced larger even-sized fields.

Further on, there is a group of buildings. This is Walcot, another settlement which was of more importance in the past. Just beyond the barn on the track, traces of medieval fishponds can be seen on the left, with earthworks in the field which are the remains of terraces, lawns and a bowling green attached to the former mansion here. The old farmhouse has an unusual steeply pitched roof.

## 12  SP349194

When the track meets the road, turn left towards Charlbury. There is a story that the avenue of scots pines lining the old turnpike road was planted in mistaken anticipation of the arrival of Bonnie Prince Charlie after the 1745 rebellion. As you cross the railway line, there is a good view of the little station, which was designed by Isambard Kingdom Brunel and is now a listed building. The walk ends at the station.

Lords and ladies

St Mary's Church, Charlbury

The Baywell

Lodge gates at entrance to Cornbury Park